Canadian Animals
Muskoxen

Laura Pratt

Weigl

Published by Weigl Educational Publishers Limited
6325 10th Street S.E.
Calgary, Alberta T2H 2Z9

www.weigl.com
Canadian Animals series © 2011
Weigl Educational Publishers Limited

Library and Archives Canada Cataloguing in Publication
Pratt, Laura, 1967-
Muskoxen / Laura Pratt.

(Canadian animals)
Includes index.
Issued also in electronic †format.
ISBN 978-1-55388-668-6 (bound).–ISBN 978-1-55388-669-3 (pbk.)

1. Muskox–Canada–Juvenile literature.
I. Title. II. Series: Canadian animals (Calgary, Alta.)

QL737.U53P73 2010 j599.64 780971 C2009-907375-7

Editor
Josh Skapin
Design
Terry Paulhus

Photograph Credits
Every reasonable effort has been made to trace ownership and to
obtain permission to reprint copyright material. The publishers would be
pleased to have any errors or omissions brought to their attention so
that they may be corrected in subsequent printings.

Weigl acknowledges Getty Images as its primary image supplier
for this title.

We gratefully acknowledge the financial support of the Government of
Canada through the Canada Book Fund for our publishing activities.

Printed in United States of America in North Mankato, Minnesota
1 2 3 4 5 6 7 8 9 0 14 13 12 11 10

062010
WEP230610

All of the Internet URLs given in the book were valid at the time of the
publication. However, due to the dynamic nature of the Internet, some
addresses may have changed, or sites may have ceased to exist since
publication. While the author and publisher regret any inconvenience
this may cause readers, no responsibility for any such changes can be
accepted by either the author or the publisher.

Contents

Meet the Muskox

The muskox is a mammal that first began living in North America between 90,000 and 200,000 years ago. Muskoxen survived the **Ice Age** and lived among woolly mammoths.

The muskox lives in the Arctic. Its body is built to help it survive the cold climate. Muskoxen can live in temperatures as cold as -40 degrees Celsius. Their thick, shaggy coat protects against freezing winds.

▶ Muskoxen live between 12 and 20 years in nature.

Muskox Facts

- Female muskoxen are called cows. Male muskoxen are called bulls.

- Bulls fight by smashing their heads together. The force of the crash is like a car driving into a concrete wall at 27 kilometres an hour.

▲ During head-on crashes, the muskox's brain is protected by an air pocket in its head.

A Very Special Animal

The muskox's outer hairs are called guard hairs. Underneath the guard hairs is a shorter, woolly coat called *qiviut*. Muskoxen shed their qiviut in the spring. New qiviut grows in summer to prepare muskoxen for winter.

In a winter storm, muskoxen form a circle to keep warm. Young muskoxen remain in the center of the circle. The big bodies of the adults shelter the young from cold winds and **predators**.

▶ Qiviut is one of the warmest furs in the world.

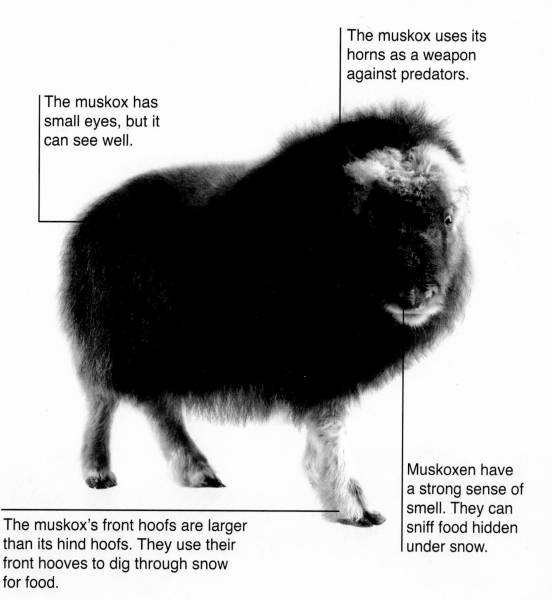

The muskox uses its horns as a weapon against predators.

The muskox has small eyes, but it can see well.

Muskoxen have a strong sense of smell. They can sniff food hidden under snow.

The muskox's front hoofs are larger than its hind hoofs. They use their front hooves to dig through snow for food.

Where Do They Live?

There are about 85,000 muskoxen in Canada. Many are found in Canada's Far North. Muskoxen also live in Greenland.

Muskoxen spend their winters on higher ground, such as hilltops. Here, they can avoid deep snow. In summer, muskoxen live in low places, such as river valleys. River valleys are where muskoxen find some of their favourite food.

▼ More than 45,000 muskoxen live in Canada's Far North.

Muskoxen Range

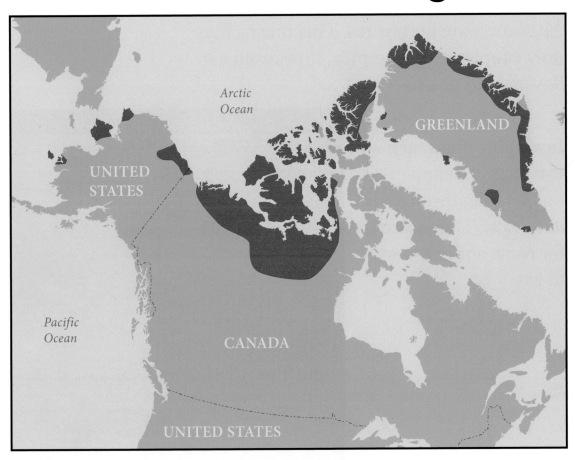

Arctic Ocean

GREENLAND

UNITED STATES

Pacific Ocean

CANADA

UNITED STATES

N
W E
S

0
0   500 Kilometres

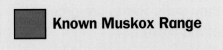

Known Muskox Range

What Do They Eat?

Muskoxen are herbivores. This means they only eat plants. In summer, muskoxen eat flowers and grass.

In winter, muskoxen use their chin and hoofs to dig through ice and snow. They search for roots and mosses to eat.

▶ Muskoxen herds eat while they walk. Herds are groups of muskoxen.

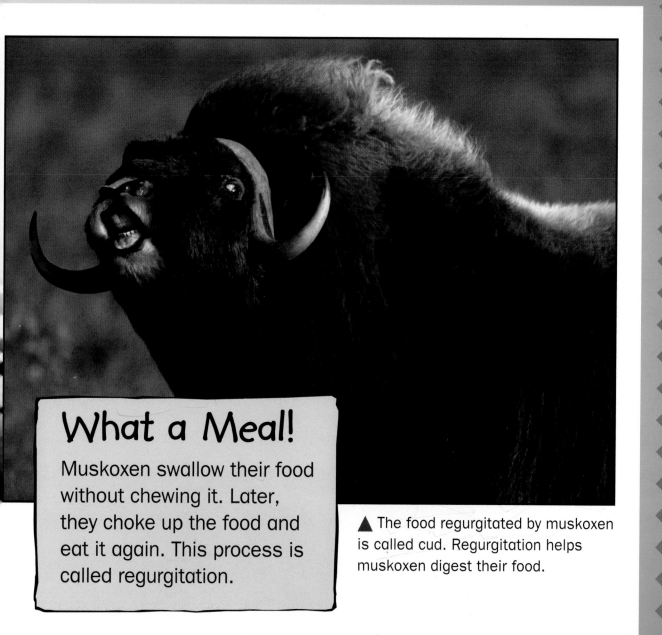

What a Meal!

Muskoxen swallow their food without chewing it. Later, they choke up the food and eat it again. This process is called regurgitation.

▲ The food regurgitated by muskoxen is called cud. Regurgitation helps muskoxen digest their food.

Making Friends

Muskoxen are social animals that live in herds. Sometimes, one female will lead a group of about 30. Herds work together to provide each other with protection from enemies.

During **calving season**, herds split into smaller groups. These smaller groups spend the summer together. Males fight with each other for the chance to mate with females. The **dominant** bull drives all other males from the herd.

▼ Herds can have as few as three muskoxen.

Muskox Talk

Muskoxen communicate by grunting, roaring, and snorting. Bulls use scents to mark their **territory**. To do this, they use a liquid that comes out of a special gland near their eyes. Muskoxen rub the liquid on the ground.

▲ Muskoxen try to prove that they are dominant to members of their herd. They do this by pushing each other and stomping the ground.

Growing Up

A baby muskox is called a calf. Female muskoxen begin having calves of their own at about age four. They can give birth to one calf each year. Calves are most often born between April and June.

The calves remain near their mothers after birth. They drink milk from their mother for about one year. Calves begin eating plants one week after birth.

▶ Muskoxen calves are born with short, woolly coats.

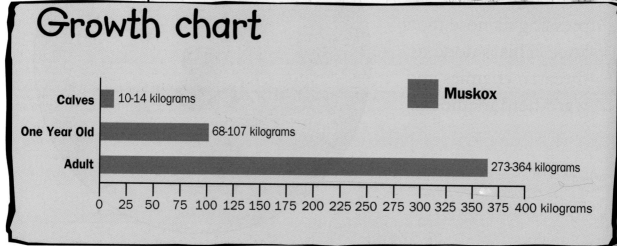

▶ Muskoxen calves are the same weight as a three-year old child.

Growth chart

Calves	10-14 kilograms
One Year Old	68-107 kilograms
Adult	273-364 kilograms

■ **Muskox**

0 25 50 75 100 125 150 175 200 225 250 275 300 325 350 375 400 kilograms

Enemies

Arctic wolves and bears are predators of the muskox. If muskoxen sense danger, the herd runs. The group then forms a circle around its young. Predators have difficulty breaking into this circle.

▼ Arctic wolves work in packs to hunt larger animals, such as muskoxen.

A threatened muskox snorts and may charge attackers. The muskox can release a musky-smelling liquid by pressing its nose to its knee. This is done to threaten enemies and warn herd members.

Comparing Sizes

Muskoxen can weigh as much as 364 kilograms. By comparison, a German shepherd dog is only about 34 kilograms.

Muskox

▲ One muskox weighs as much as 11 German shepherd dogs.

Under Threat

Humans are the biggest threat to muskoxen. They hunt these animals for their hides and meat. Muskoxen were once overhunted by European settlers. As a result, they almost became **extinct**. In 1917, the Canadian government made a law to protect muskoxen from being hunted. Now, there are between 100,000 and 150,000 muskoxen in the world.

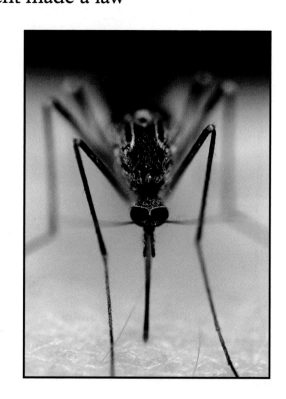

Diseases carried by mosquitoes can be a threat to muskoxen. Female mosquitoes spread disease when they pierce the animal's skin to drink its blood.

▶ Blood is needed to help mosquitoes produce eggs.

► Coal-fired power stations create a great deal of pollution.

What Do You Think?

Scientists have found pollution in Arctic air and water. This pollution can be a threat to Arctic animals, including muskoxen. Pollution can be caused by industries, such as the power industry. What do you think can be done to decrease pollution in the Arctic?

Myths and Legends

There are many names for muskoxen. Often, these names refer to fur around the animal's head, which looks like a beard. Aboriginal Peoples call muskoxen *omingmak*. This word means "animal with skin like a beard."

Aboriginal Peoples have many stories about muskoxen. In an Inuit story, two muskoxen sing about the beauty of the land. The muskoxen are later hunted. The hunters then steal the muskoxen's song for themselves.

▼ In Greenland, muskoxen are called *umimmak*. This means "long-bearded one."

Aboriginal Peoples tell a story about how the weasel helped hungry animals by hunting a muskox. In the story, there is no food for the animals to eat. A fox finds a muskox and tells a wolf to hunt it for the meat. The wolf says he is not strong enough. A weasel says he will hunt the muskox, and all the animals laugh. The weasel was a hero. He brought back enough muskox meat to feed all the animals.

▲ Weasels most often hunt smaller animals, such as field mice and frogs.

Quiz

1. Muskoxen shed their qiviut in
(a) **the fall** (b) **the summer** (c) **the spring**

2. Muskoxen survive the Canadian winters due to
(a) **their keen eyesight** (b) **their warm coat**
(c) **their ability to light campfires**

3. A muskoxen baby is called
(a) **a pup** (b) **a kid** (c) **a calf**

4. What animal is a muskox's
greatest enemy?
(a) **Arctic wolf** (b) **Arctic rabbit**
(c) **Arctic fox**

Answers:
1. (c) Muskoxen shed their qiviut in the spring.
2. (b) A muskoxen's warm coat helps it survive Canadian winters.
3. (c) A muskoxen baby is called a calf.
4. (a) A muskox's greatest enemy is the Arctic wolf.

Find out More

To find out more about muskoxen, visit these websites.

Nunavut Muskox
www.nunavutmuskox.ca

Hinterland Who's Who
www.hww.ca/hww2.asp?id=95

Tundra Animals
www.tundraanimals.net/guide/muskox.html

Words to Know

calving season
the time of year when muskoxen
give birth

dominant
stronger than the others

extinct
no longer living on Earth

Ice Age
a period of time about 20,000 years
ago when huge ice sheets covered large
parts of the North America, Europe,
and Asia

predators
animals that hunt other animals for food

territory
the area where an animal lives and looks
for food

Index